Learn About Plants!

Flowers

By

Steffi Cavell-Clarke

KidHaven
PUBLISHING

Published in 2018 by
KidHaven Publishing, an Imprint of Greenhaven Publishing, LLC
353 3rd Avenue
Suite 255
New York, NY 10010

© 2018 Booklife Publishing
This edition is published by arrangement with Booklife Publishing.

Designer: Danielle Jones
Editor: Charlie Ogden

Cataloging-in-Publication Data

Names: Cavell-Clarke, Steffi.
Title: Flowers / Steffi Cavell-Clarke.
Description: New York : KidHaven Publishing, 2018. | Series: Learn about plants! | Includes index.
Identifiers: ISBN 9781534522435 (pbk.) | ISBN 9781534522398 (library bound) | ISBN 9781534522312 (6 pack) | ISBN 9781534522350 (ebook)
Subjects: LCSH: Flowers–Juvenile literature. | Plant anatomy–Juvenile literature.
Classification: LCC QK49.C38 2018 | DDC 580–dc23

Printed in the United States of America

CPSIA compliance information: Batch #BS17KL: For further information contact Greenhaven Publishing LLC, New York, New York at 1-844-317-7404.

Please visit our website, www.greenhavenpublishing.com. For a free color catalog of all our high-quality books, call toll free 1-844-317-7404 or fax 1-844-317-7405.

PHOTO CREDITS

Abbreviations: l-left, r-right, b-bottom, t-top, c-center, m-middle.

Front cover – VICUSCHKA, Denise Torres, Julia Ardaran, Evgeny Karandaev, david156, Zoteva. 1 – italianestro. 2– Sunny studio. 4 – Romolo Tavani. 4br – GongTo. 5 main – amenic181. 5lm – Elena Elisseeva. 6 main – Mizuri. 6cr – Ragnarock. 7 main – Andrii Muzyka. 7tl – Pratchaya.Lee. 7ml – MongPro. 7bl – Veselka. 8l – Ian 2010. 8ml – pukach. 8mr – Silver Spiral Arts. 8r – Silver Spiral Arts. 9 – Ian Grainger. 10 – olgaman. 11bl – Monika Gniot. 11m – Passakorn sakulphan. 11r – sakhorn. 12 main – fullempty. 12cr – Tischenko Irina. 13 main – alybaba. 13tl – pjhpix. 13mr – Robsonphoto. 13br – Maxal Tamor. 14 – Leena Robinson. 15 – Dave Montreuil. 16 main – Nailia Schwarz. 16cr – Tsekhmister. 17 main – SweetCrisis. 17tl – Igor Sokolov (breeze). 17ml – StevenRussellSmithPhotos. 17bl – all_about_people. 18 – Tropper2000. 19 – Monika Gniot. 20 main – Elena Elisseeva. 20cr – Sandra van der Steen. 21 main – Johnny Adolphson. 21tl – Raymond Llewellyn. 21mr – Svetlana Lukienko. 21br – Pippa Sanderson. 22 – kkaplin. 23 – Peera_stockfoto.
Images are courtesy of Shutterstock.com, with thanks to Getty Images, Thinkstock Photo, and iStockphoto.

CONTENTS

Words that look like **this** can be found in the glossary on page 24.

What Is a Plant?

A plant is a living thing. All living things need water, air, and **sunlight** to live.

There are many different kinds of plants. Most plants have roots, leaves, flowers, and a stem.

Plants live all around the world!

What Is a Flower?

A flower is a part of a plant that grows from the stem.

Flowers have many important jobs to do. They make pollen and seeds, which are needed to make new plants.

What Do **Flowers** Look Like?

sunflower

rose

tulip

daffodil

Flowers come in many different shapes and sizes.

Flowers are often bright and colorful. They often have a sweet smell, too. This helps them **attract** insects.

Bees like **nectar**, which can be found in flowers.

9

How Do **Flowers** Grow?

Most plants grow one or more flower heads. In order to grow, the flower heads need water, air, and sunlight.

A flower starts as a small bud that grows from the stem of a plant. When it is fully grown, the bud opens up into a flower.

flower

flower bud

Parts of a Flower

Flowers have many different parts, such as petals. The petals help **protect** the other parts of the flower.

In the center of a flower are the stamens and the stigma. The stamens make the pollen. The stigma receives the pollen.

stigma

stamen

13

What Do Flowers Do?

Butterflies are attracted to colorful petals.

A flower's job is to attract insects and other animals using its bright colors and sweet smells.

14

Insects and other animals feed on the nectar flowers make.

This butterfly is drinking nectar from a flower.

15

When an insect visits a flower to drink its nectar, the flower's pollen sticks to its body.

16

The pollen then falls off on the next flower the insect visits.

This bee has pollen stuck to its body.

17

Once a flower has taken in pollen from another flower, it can make seeds.

18

Some seeds are blown away by the wind and become buried in soil. Once seeds have enough water and sunlight, they grow into new plants.

19

Flowers in the Garden

A gardener can water plants to help the flowers grow.

Many people like to grow flowers in their gardens.

There are also many flowers that grow in the wild. These are called wildflowers. Daffodils, bluebells, and daisies are often found growing in the wild.

Strange Flowers

Rafflesia arnoldii

Not all flowers smell nice. *Rafflesia arnoldii* is the largest flower on Earth. It smells like rotting meat to attract flies!

The black bat flower has black petals that make it look like a bat!

black bat flower

23

GLOSSARY

attract to make something come closer
grow to naturally develop and increase in size
nectar a sweet liquid found in flowers
pollen a powder-like substance made by flowers
protect to keep safe
soil the upper layer of the earth where plants grow
sunlight light from the sun

INDEX

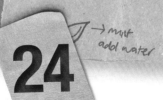